# Written by Patrick Geistdoerfer
# Illustrated by Joëlle Boucher

*Specialist adviser:*
*Andy Ottaway, Whale Campaigner,*
*Greenpeace*

*ISBN 1 85103 101 4*
*First published 1990 in the United Kingdom*
*by Moonlight Publishing Ltd,*
*36 Stratford Road, London W8*
*Translated by Sarah Gibson*

POCKET • WORLDS

# Whales, Dolphins
## and Seals

There are giants in our oceans . . .

In the Bible story of Jonah and the whale, Jonah is thrown overboard by his shipmates and swallowed by a great fish.

After three days and nights in the fish's stomach, Jonah is thrown up safe and sound on dry land.

Can you think of other stories about someone who is swallowed by a whale? What about Pinocchio?

Fish breathe in the water, lay eggs and are cold-blooded. **Whales and dolphins are mammals, not fish.** That means they swim to the surface to breathe air and are warm-blooded. They give birth to live young and feed them with milk. They never come up on to dry land,

Stone Age man made pictures of dolphins.

A dolphin painted in Crete 4,000 years ago

though! Like fish, they spend their whole lives in the water. They belong to a group of mammals called **cetaceans,** specially adapted to life in the sea.

Long ago, people believed whales were dangerous and terrifying sea-monsters!

Whales are so enormous that people used to be frightened of them. But whales are gentle giants and they do not hurt people.

Dolphins are much smaller. They often swim close to shore or circle playfully around boats at sea, unafraid of the sailors.

A god is riding on a dolphin's back in this picture from Ancient Greece.

**Few of the largest whales have teeth.**
Instead they have a fringe of horny plates
called baleen, which helps them filter
their food.

Bowhead whale

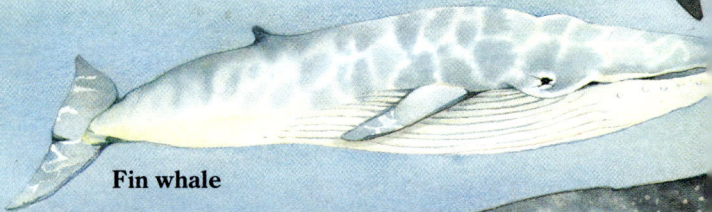

Fin whale

Blue whale

The baleen plates hang down in rows from the top of the whale's mouth. Some whales have as many as 3,000 plates, measuring 3 metres long!

**Humpback whale**

**Great right whale**

# All the other cetaceans have teeth.

Some cetaceans are enormous, like the sperm whale. Others, like porpoises and dolphins, are much smaller.

**Dolphins**

**Killer whale**

The narwhal has just one long tooth, like a horn, which it uses to defend itself.

The beluga is dark grey when it is born, then its skin becomes mottled. Four or five years later, it is completely white.

**Sperm whale**

**Beluga, or white whale**

Cetaceans are found in all the oceans of the world. In summer some migrate to the colder oceans where food is more plentiful. During winter, they move to warmer seas to give birth to their young.

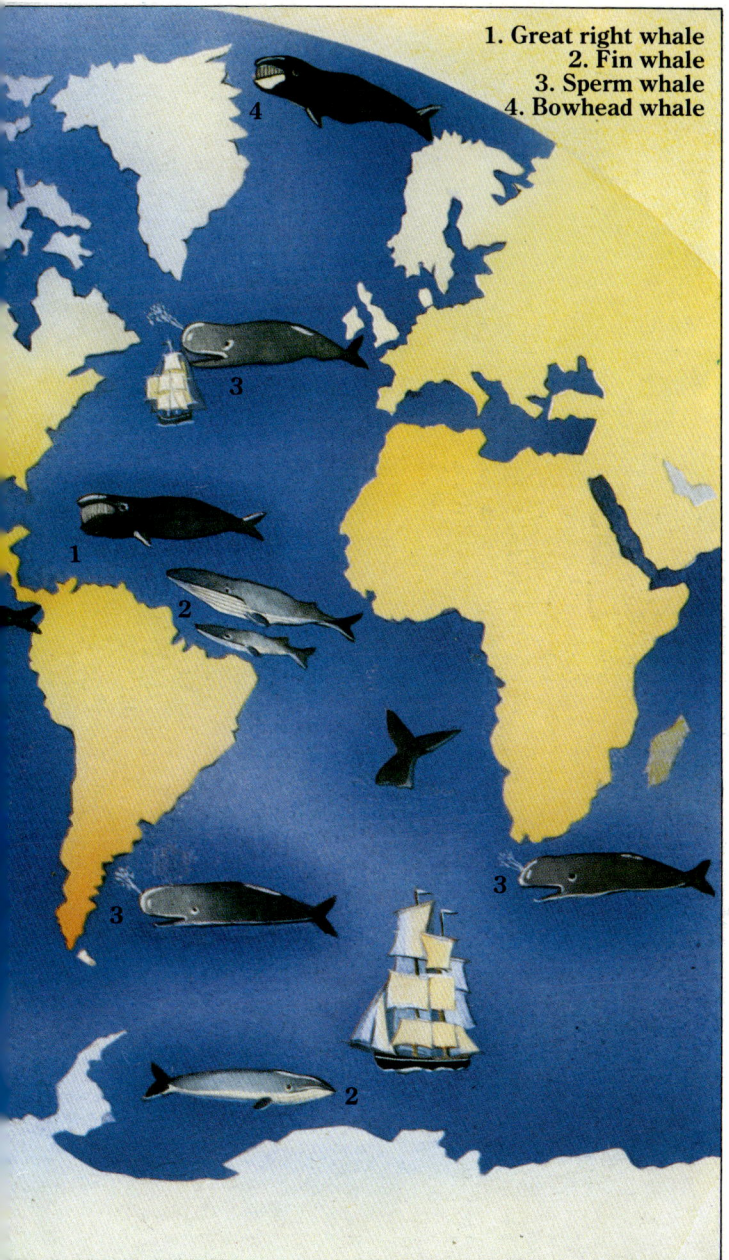

1. Great right whale
2. Fin whale
3. Sperm whale
4. Bowhead whale

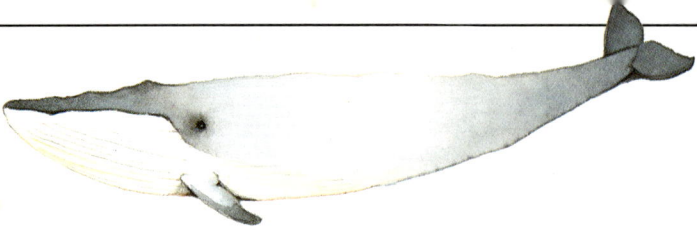

**The blue whale is the largest and heaviest animal in the world.** Some blue whales are 30 metres long, the length of four coaches parked one behind the other. They can weigh as much as thirty elephants – more than 130 tonnes.

The blue whale's tongue alone is as heavy as an elephant! The sperm whale and the right whale are each about 20 metres long. The dolphin is smaller: just 2 or 3 metres from nose to tail. It's still a giant compared to us!

The biggest animal on land is the elephant. It weighs about 4 tonnes and can be up to 4 metres tall.

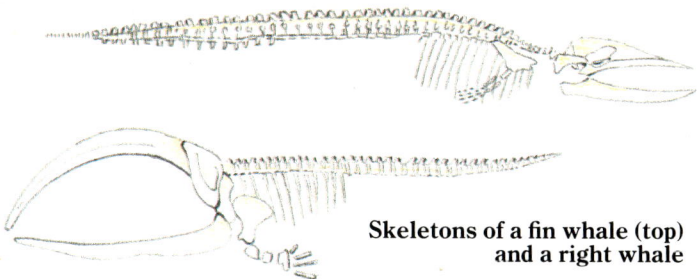

Skeletons of a fin whale (top)
and a right whale

Look at these skeletons. A whale has two flippers where we have arms, but the bones are very similar to our own. Whales and dolphins swim by moving their powerful tails up and down, not from side to side like a fish.

**Their skin is thin and smooth.**

Underneath it is a thick layer of fat, called blubber, which helps to keep them warm. It also acts as a food store on their long journeys through the oceans.

**How do whales breathe?**

Through one or two nostrils or blow-holes on top of their heads. They swim to the surface and blow a cloud of steamy stale air from their lungs up into the air above the sea. This blow is the first clue that there is a whale nearby!

A whale blowing

The dorsal fin of
a killer whale

The tail of a blue whale

Whales and dolphins live in family groups called schools. Sometimes there are several hundred living together, with one animal acting as leader.

## Why do they leap out of the water?

To raise the alarm, to keep in contact in rough seas, or sometimes to attract females. The young do it just for fun!

Here is a whale doing a most complicated manoeuvre. It turns in the air before landing on its back with a terrific splash!

When large whales leap out of the water it is called breaching.

All cetaceans dive, and they can stay deep underwater for a very long time.

A dolphin can swim very fast, at speeds of up to 50 k.p.h. It leaps out of the water to take breaths of air as it swims along.

The sperm whale holds the record for diving. It can swim down more than two kilometres below the surface, and stay underwater for an hour and a half!

Birth of a dolphin calf

Carried on its mother's back

## The biggest baby in the world!

The calf of a blue whale develops inside its mother for 10 months. At birth, it weighs 5 tonnes and is 7 metres long. Its mother has to coax it to the surface to take its first vital breaths.

The female dolphin suckles her calf for 16 months.

## All whale calves are suckled by their mothers underwater.

The milk squirts straight into their mouths from their mother's teats. A newborn calf drinks up to 450 litres of milk every day. The calf doubles its birth weight in only a week, growing at the rate of 4.5 kg every hour! It builds up a thick layer of blubber which protects it from the cold. Dolphins live for 20 or 30 years, while whales may live till they are over 50.

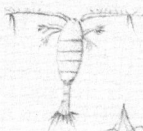

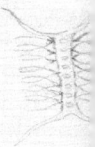

The blue whale eats nearly a thousand kilos of tiny animals in a single meal.

## What do these ocean giants eat?

Whales without teeth cannot swallow large chunks of food. They feed on small fish and plankton, tiny animals and plants floating in the sea. The whale takes a mouthful of sea-water and then uses its tongue to force the water out again, trapping the plankton inside against the fringe of baleen, which acts as a sort of strainer.

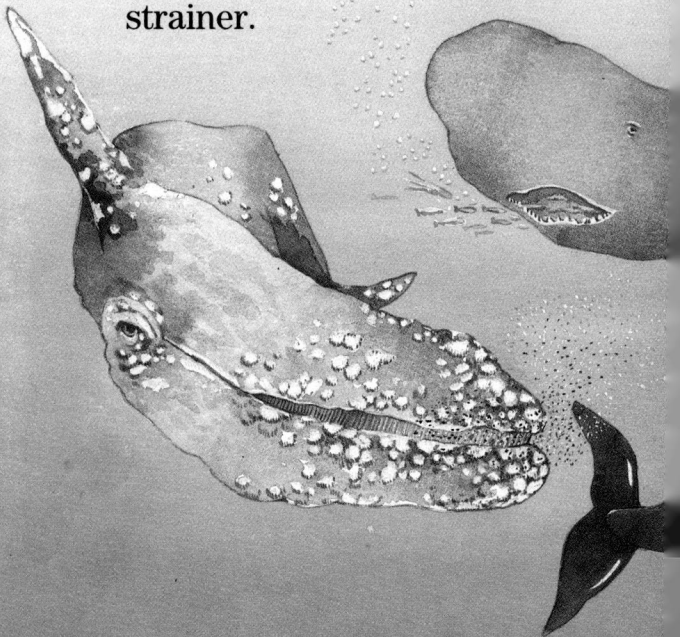

Sperm whales feed on squid and fish, which they swallow whole.

Toothed whales and dolphins live mainly on fish and squid. A squid can grow quite large, with long tentacles, and the biggest ones put up quite a fight! But it's not an equal match – the squid always ends up in the whale's stomach!

Killer whales are not whales at all, but a sort of large dolphin. **Swimming in packs like wolves of the sea, killer whales are expert hunters!** Their large dorsal fins slice through the surface of the water as they search for

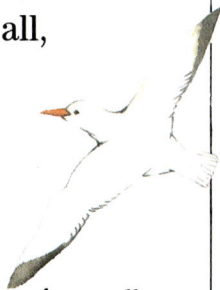

A seagull

sharks, seals, dolphins and birds, as well as for squid and fish.

They may even attack a large whale, which does not stand a chance against these agile killers with their fearsome rows of teeth.

A seal

A killer whale has a huge appetite. Scientists found the remains of 11 seals and 13 porpoises in the stomach of a single whale!

But killer whales have a reputation they do not deserve; they do not attack people.

A dolphin

**Dolphins are very intelligent.** They can be trained to help divers fetch objects from the ocean bed, and are quick to learn tricks based on their natural movements, like balancing upright on their tails or leaping through hoops. You may have seen tame killer whales or dolphins performing at an aquarium. They are great fun to watch, but they are not happy and do not live long in captivity.

**Dolphins and whales have their own language.** They send out a variety of sounds to communicate with each other: whistles, groans, chirps and clicks. Sailors even talk about whales singing! Dolphins and toothed whales have poor eyesight, but they can hear very well. Like bats, they use sound to tell them if there is something in their way. The returning echo tells them the shape of the object and how far away it is.

**Why have people hunted whales for so long?** In the past, the body of a whale provided lots of things humans found useful. The blubber was melted down to

provide oil. Before electricity, whale oil was used as fuel in lamps, and was made into soap and margarine. The baleen, also known as whalebone, was used to make the spokes of umbrellas and the stiffening in ladies' corsets. A white, waxy substance in the skull of sperm whales was used to oil wristwatches and gearboxes. And the meat is good to eat.

Cutting up
a stranded
whale

At first, people just took advantage of whales that were stranded on the beach, but soon they began to hunt them from boats all over the world.

**Hunting a whale used to be very dangerous.** If it jumped, or brought its huge tail crashing down, the whale could smash the boat to pieces and the sailors would drown.

Great right whale

Blue whale

Fin whale

Humpback whale

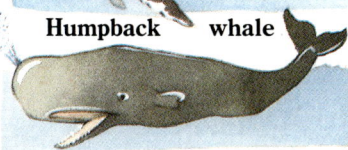

Sperm whale

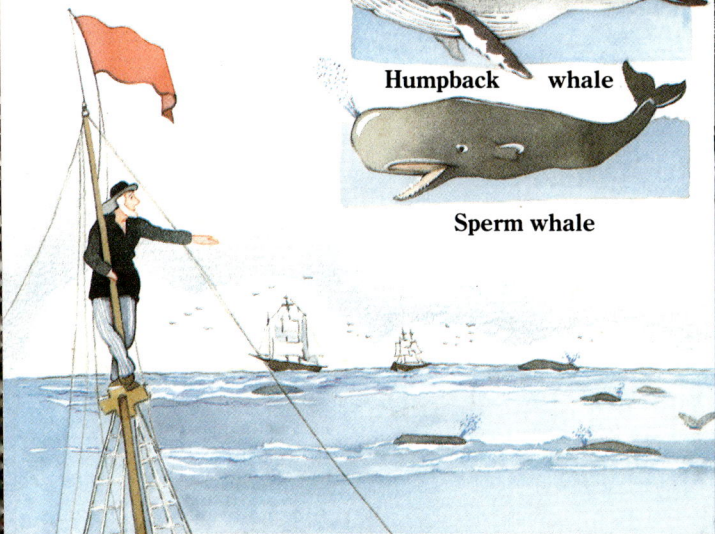

**From high on the mast, the sailor on watch shouted 'There she blows!'** That was the signal for the whole crew to get ready. They set out in small, light whale-boats, rowing as fast as they could towards the whale. The harpooner stood at the front, his harpoon tied to the boat by a long line.

As soon as the whale-boat was close enough, the sailor hurled his harpoon deep into the whale's body. The wounded animal, struggling to escape, dived down and swam as fast as it could, dragging the whale-boat behind it. The chase could last for hours. But in the end, the whale grew tired and the sailors where able to kill it with thrusts from their spears.

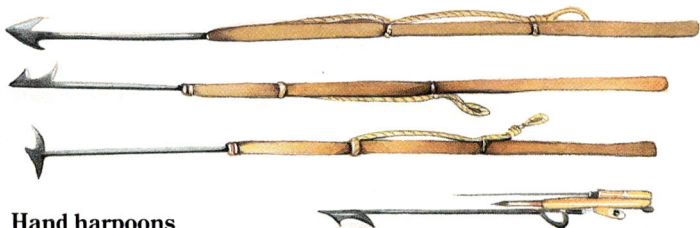
Hand harpoons

In some parts of the world, sailors waited on land for the whales to appear. Look-outs were posted on the high points of the islands, and signalled if they caught sight of a sperm whale. At once the whale-boats, lying in readiness on the beaches, were put to sea. Once the whale had been killed it was tied alongside or towed behind one of the boats, back to the shore. The whale's blubber was cut up into strips and melted down in cauldrons, and the oil made from it was stored in small barrels.

Carving on a sperm whale's tooth

A 19th-century whaling-vessel

## Modern whaling is very different.

Powerful ships, 30 or 40 metres long, set out in fleets. At the front of each ship is a harpoon-cannon. The cannon fires a shell which explodes when it hits the whale, mortally wounding it. The catcher-ships tow their prize back to the waiting factory-ship, where the whale is hoisted on board through an opening in the back of the ship, and cut up in pieces. The whales do not stand a chance against these modern hunting methods.

A catcher-ship drags its prey alongside.

The factory-ship hoists the whale on board, where it is tied fast to the deck.

## Over 2 million whales have been killed this century.

There is now a world-wide ban on killing whales, but some countries, like Japan, Norway and Iceland, continue to hunt them in large numbers. Today all great whales are endangered.

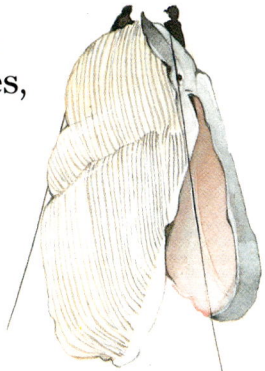

# Let's not forget some other mammals which live in the sea!

A sea-lion's ears are on the outside of its head. A seal's are not.

Seals and their cousins spend part of their lives on land or on ice-floes. They can stay underwater for up to twenty minutes. Their skin is covered with short, sleek fur, and they eat fish, crabs, shell-fish and sea-birds. The biggest of these animals is the sea-elephant, which can weigh more than 4 tonnes, and may measure 5 metres from nose to tail.

The walrus has huge tusks which it uses to dig for shellfish on the sea-bottom and to haul itself on to ice-floes.

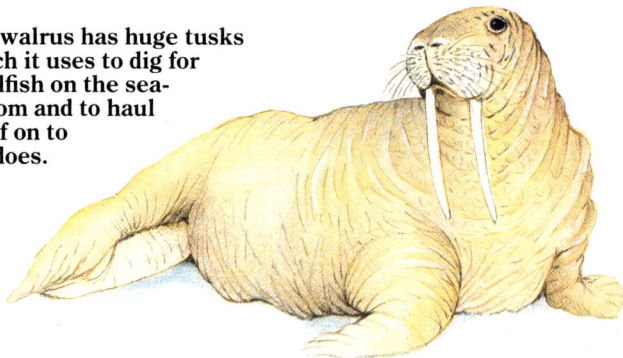

The monk seal lives in
the Mediterranean Sea.

The smallest seal is the
ringed seal.

The grey seal lives off
the coasts of Britain.

The male elephant seal can inflate
his nose like a trunk!

The hooded seal lives in
icy polar waters.

The male can
inflate his nose, too.

# Index